This Book Belongs To:

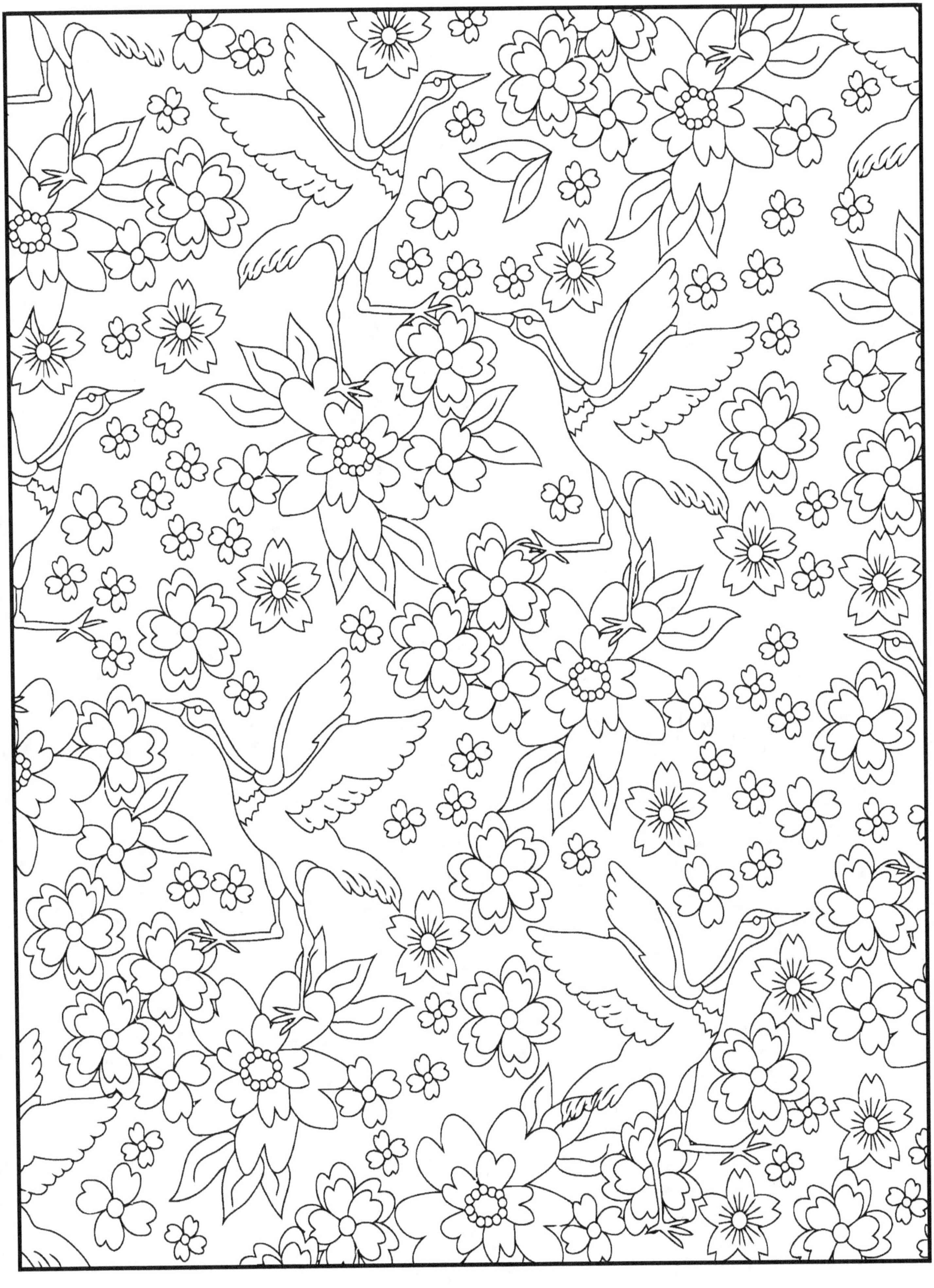

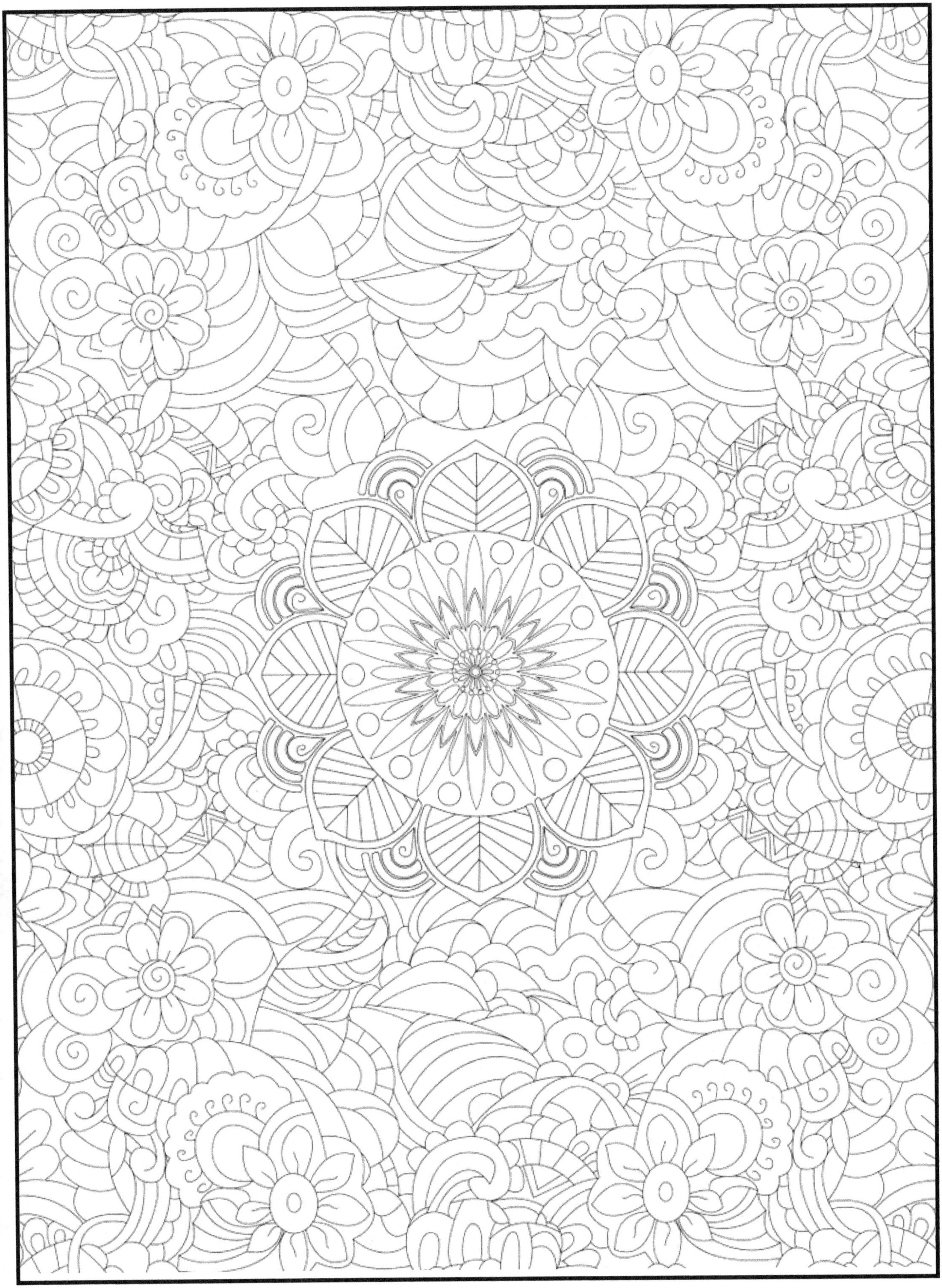

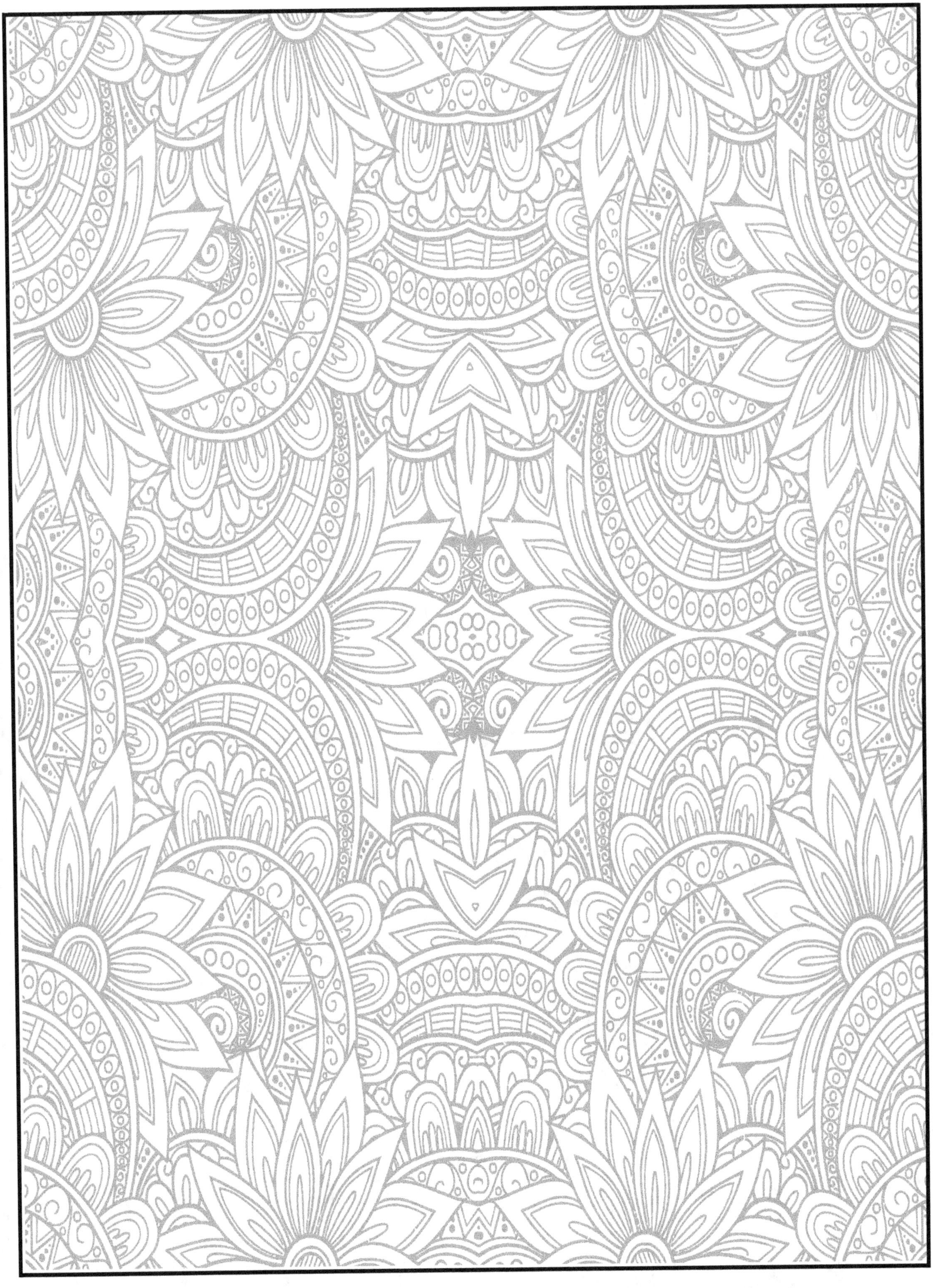

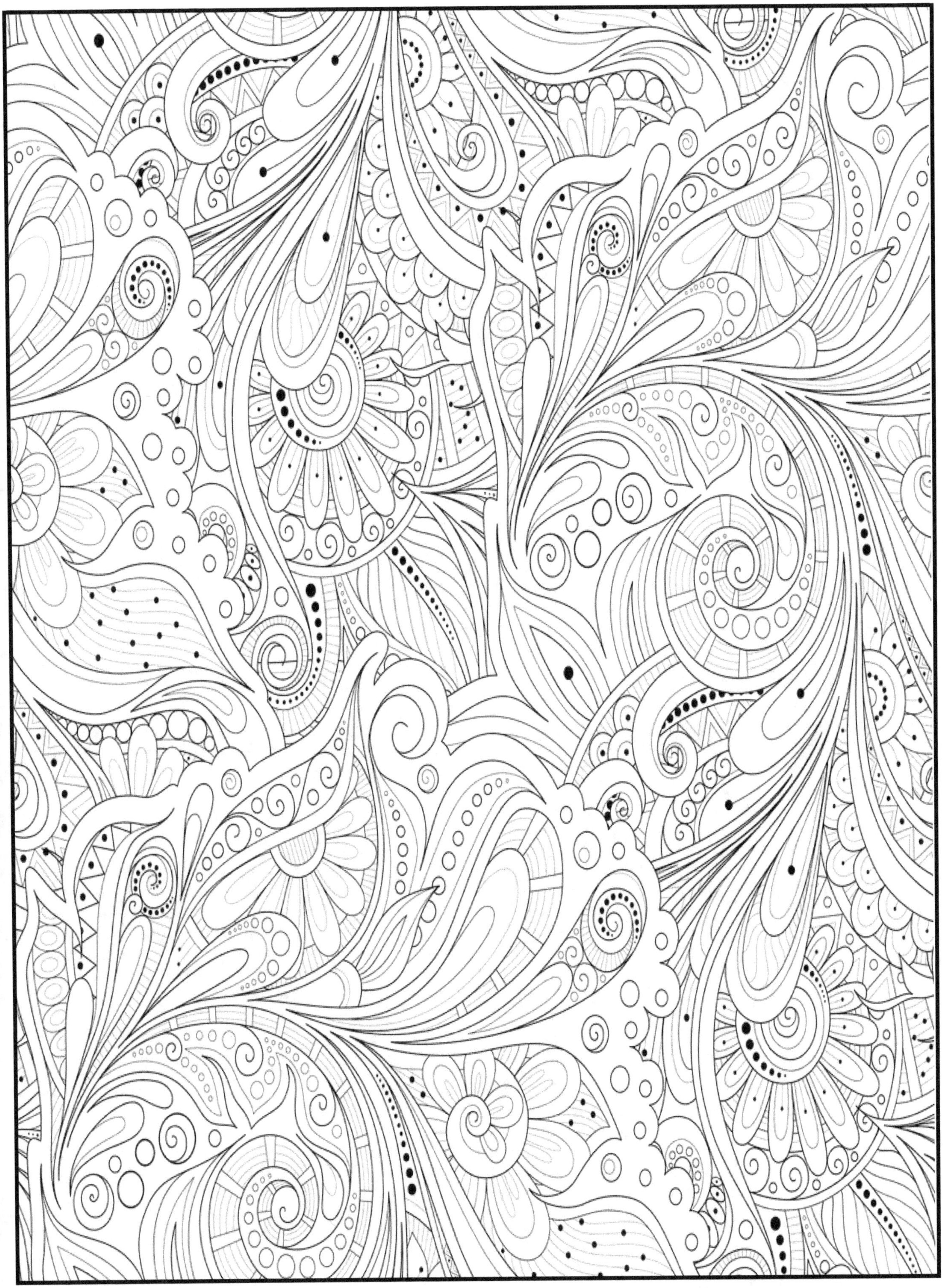

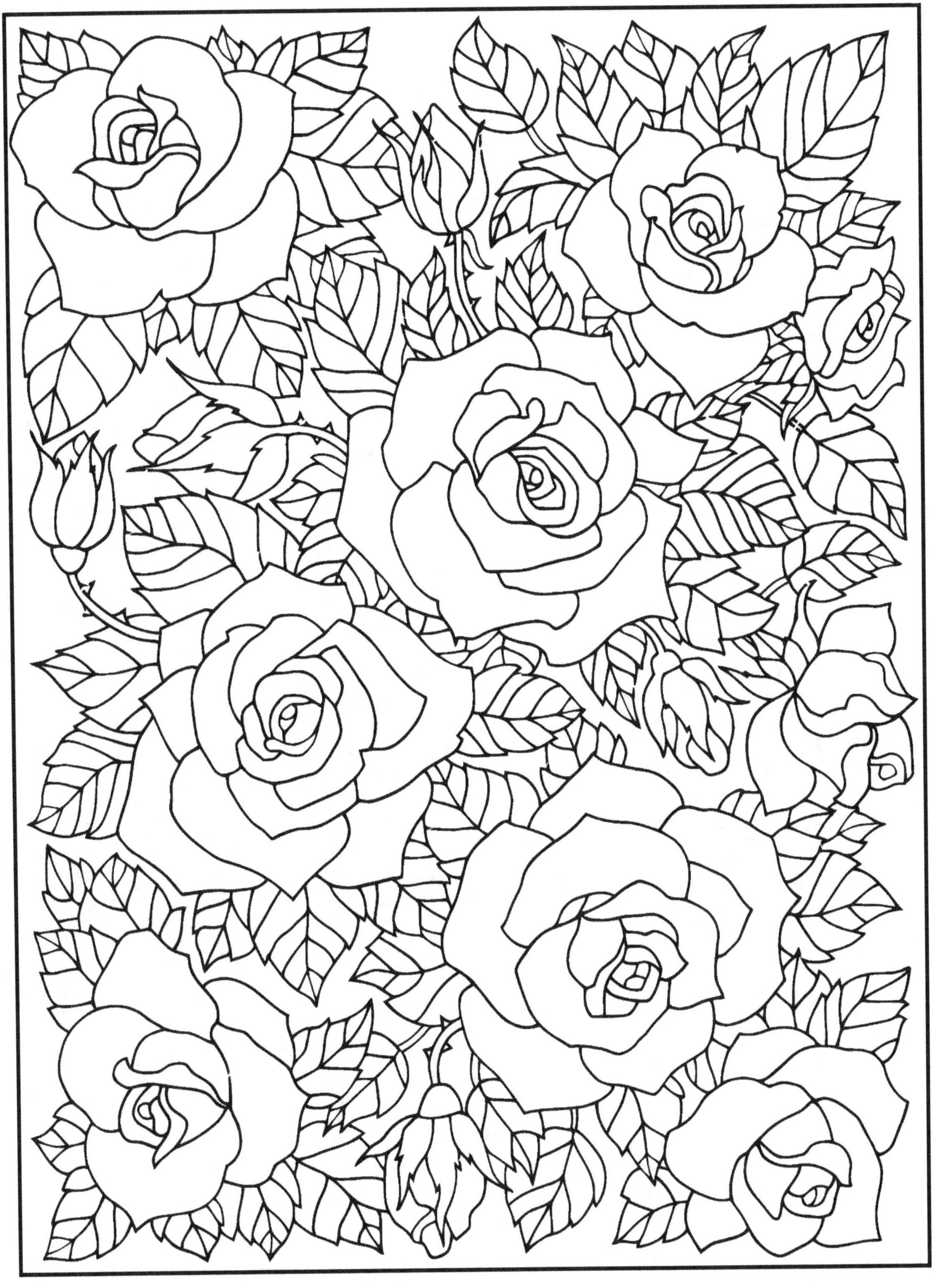

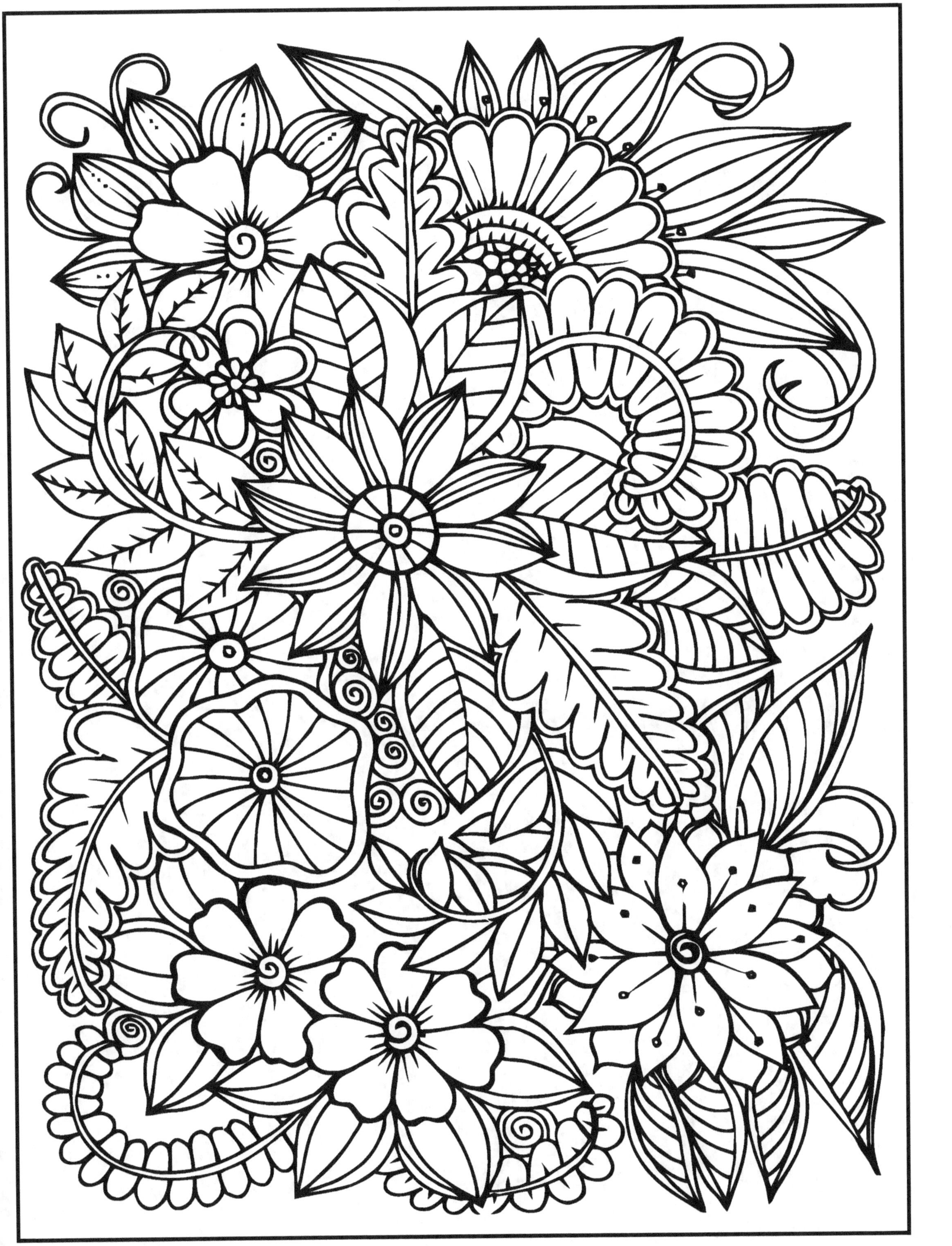

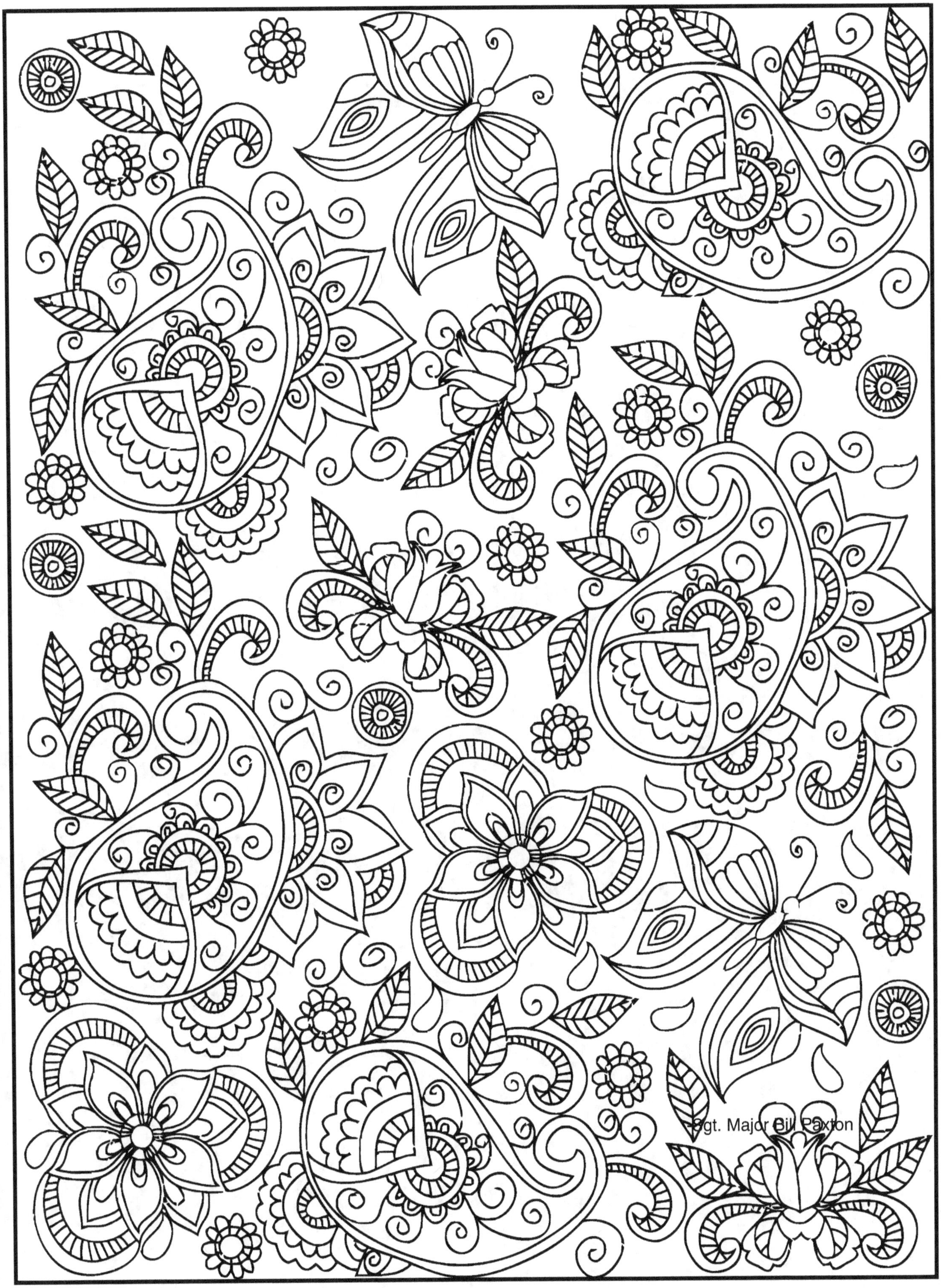
Sgt. Major Bill Paxton

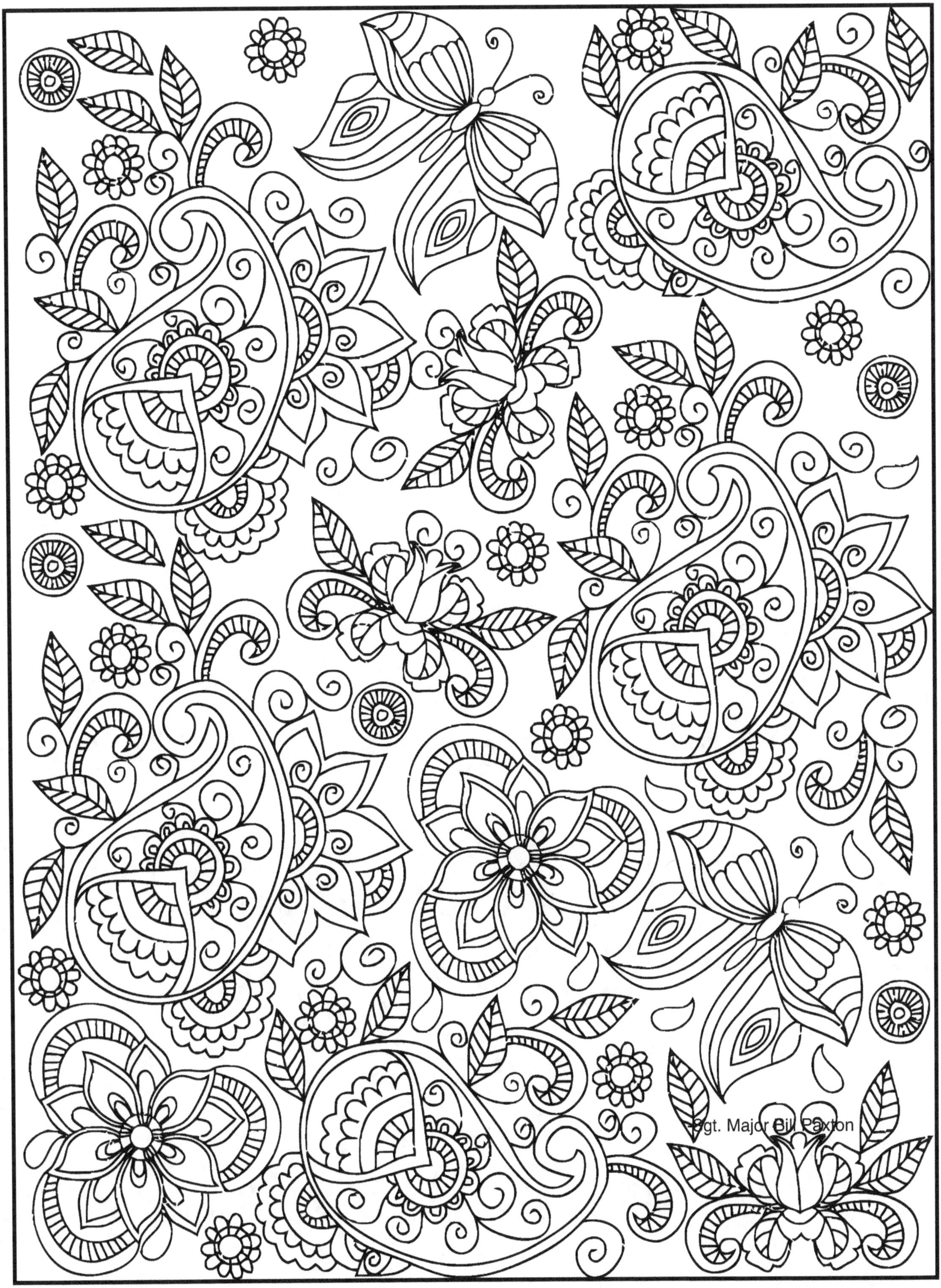
Sgt. Major Bill Paxton

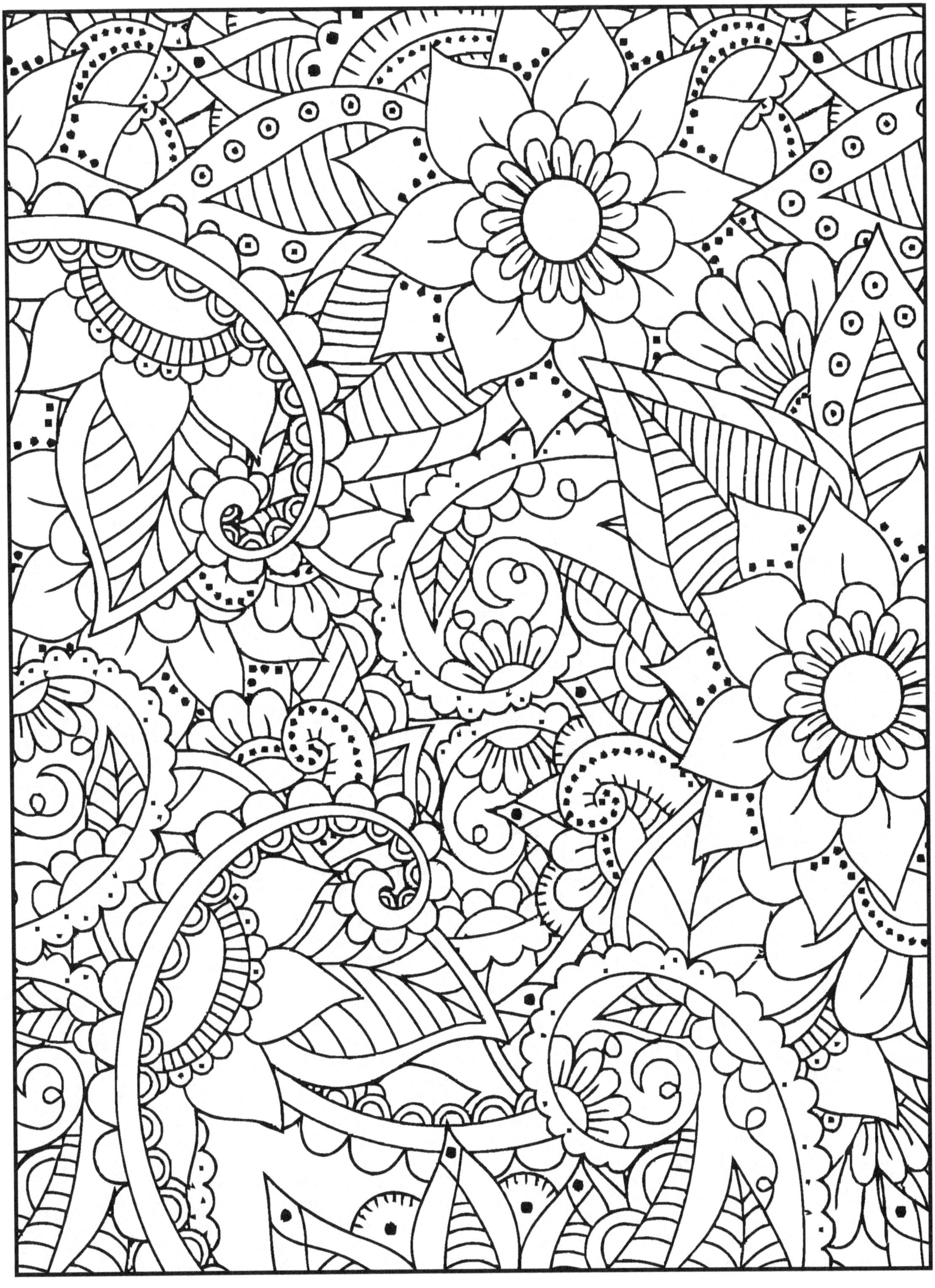

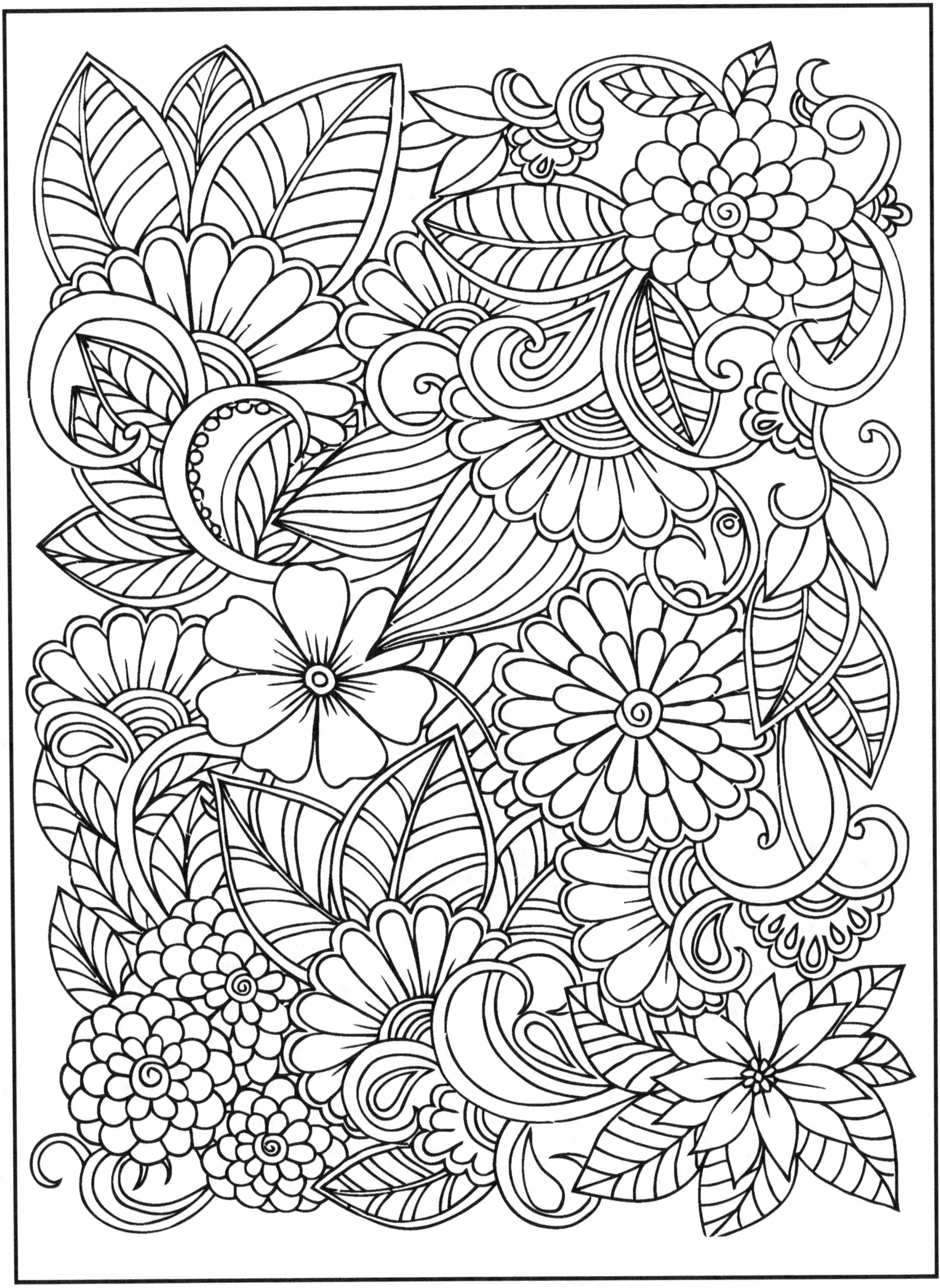

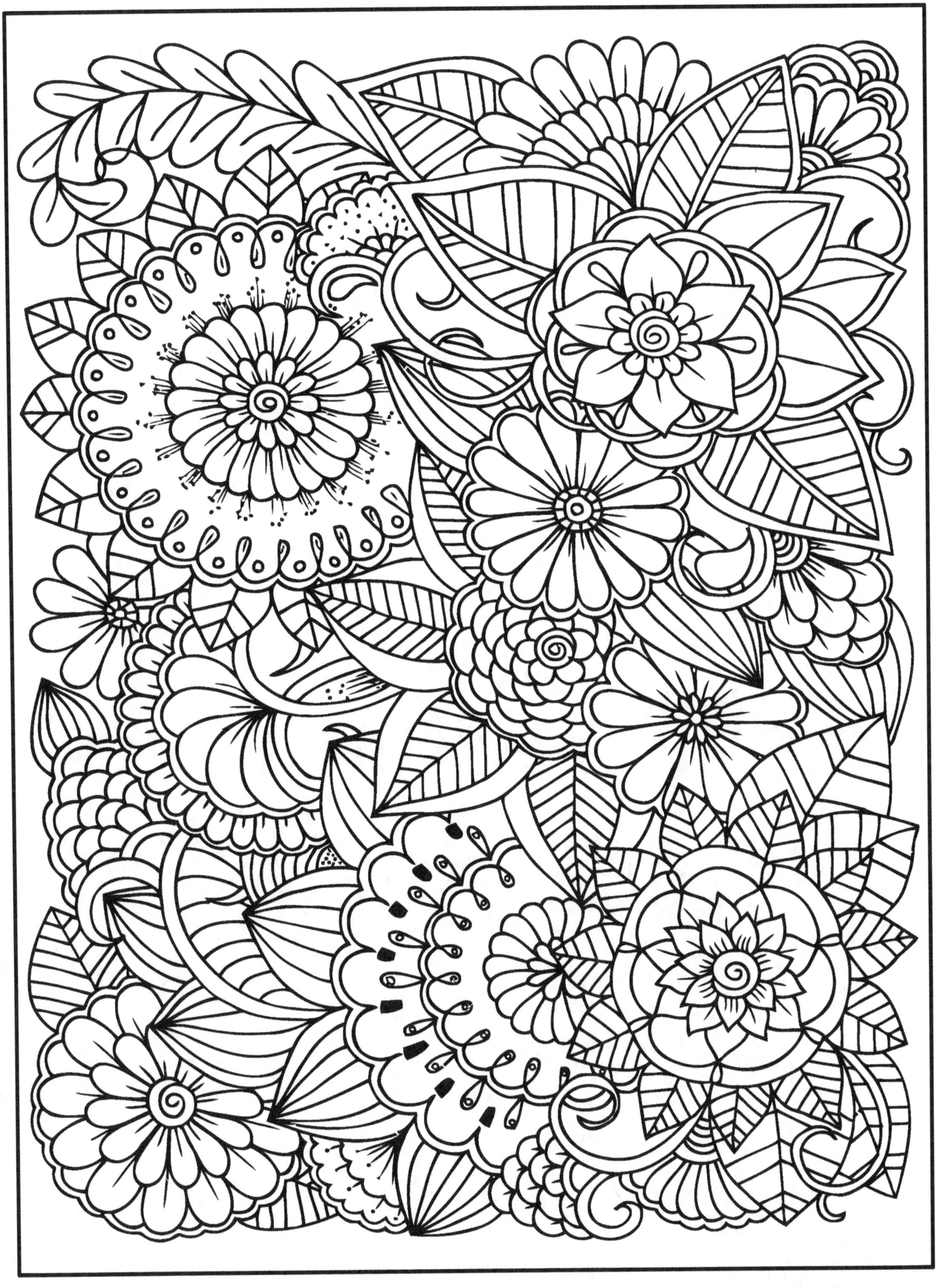

www.ingramcontent.com/pod-product-compliance
Lightning Source LLC
Chambersburg PA
CBHW081101240526
45465CB00025B/2809